The POTTER'S

Project Book

Burnished pots by Peter Cosentino

Non-functional pieces of work still have links with the
techniques involved in work of a more practical nature.
These composite pots were speckled with different colour
slips and burnished before firing.

The POTTER'S Project Book

PETER COSENTINO

WINDWARD

First published in Great Britain in 1987 by Windward

An imprint owned by W.H. Smith & Sons Limited
Registered No 237811 England
Trading as WHS Distributors
St. John's House, East Street, Leicester LE1 6NE

First impression 1987
Copyright © 1987 The Paul Press Limited
All rights reserved.

ISBN 0-7112-0446-2

Typeset by AKM Associates (U.K.) Ltd.,
Ajmal House, Hayes Road, Southall, London UB2 5NG
Origination by South Sea International, Hong Kong
Printed in the UK through
Print Buyer's Database Ltd

This book was edited, designed and produced by
The Paul Press Ltd., 22, Bruton Street, London W1X 7DA

Art Editor	Antony Johnson
Project Editor	Emma Warlow
Editorial	Vicky Waters
Photography	David Sheppard
Line illustrations	Hayward & Martin Ltd., Ian Bott
Index	Kathy Gill

Art Director	Stephen McCurdy
Managing Editor	Elizabeth Longley
Editorial Director	Jeremy Harwood
Publishing Director	Nigel Perryman

Contents

Foreword

This book is dedicated to my wife Mandy, and to
Thomas and Matthew, my two sons. I would like to
thank Emma, Antony and Vicky from The Paul Press
for helping to make working on this book such a
happy experience, and my special thanks must go to
David Sheppard, the photographer whose sensitive
work has contributed so much to the projects.

Anyone who has watched an experienced thrower at
work cannot fail to be amazed by the almost magical
ease with which the successive vessels seem to flow
from his fingers. In reality, of course, a potter's
confidence and masterful skill stem from years of
patient practice and determined hard work. It would
be foolish to suggest that a beginner can achieve the
same results; nevertheless, competent throwing is
well within the reach of anyone who is prepared to
put effort into learning the basic skills and
techniques. Many students surprise themselves with
the quality of their first efforts.

In this book, I have tried to plan projects of varying
complexity, so that both the beginner and the more
advanced potter can enjoy making all sorts of
attractive and functional pieces of pottery that stretch
their personal ability. It is also designed to provide
busy pottery teachers with a solution when their
pupils have grasped the basics of throwing and need
a range of new challenges to keep them occupied.

There are never enough pages in any book to cover
all the information that the author wants to convey.
The Potter's Project Book is no exception. Although I
would be the first to acknowledge the importance of
considering the complete design process from the
first stages of planning, through construction and
decoration, to glazing and firing, the true concern of
this book is the actual business of throwing. I have
therefore explained the decorative technique of using
textured rollers to imprint the clay, because it is
undertaken during throwing rather than when the
form has dried. Like all the suggested decoration, this
technique can be used on any of the projects in the
book. The other techniques and the types of glaze

that should be used to create the specific effects
illustrated are briefly outlined at the end of each
project. All these projects have been fired to
a temperature of 1250°C in an electric kiln.

There is never any one correct way to make a
particular item. No matter what the basic criteria are
that determine the basic styling of any functional
piece of pottery, (such as ease of handling, steadiness
and durability), they can all be fulfilled in completely
different ways. Two casseroles, for instance, can have
differing lid fittings and handles and be made from
very different clays, yet they will both be just as
efficient. Throughout the book, I have tried to
emphasize that my way is not necessarily the best,
and is certainly not the only, way to make any of the
projects I have covered. The techniques I employed
were those that I find the easiest, and are therefore
recommended as a starting point for the
development of your own personal style and
technique — which is after all the central aim of the
book. The development of an indvidual style can only
progress from the gradual exploration of personal
ideas and technique. With this in mind, **The Potter's
Project Book** has been designed to stimulate
creativity and to provide the reader with a sound
guide on which to base his experimentation.

Pottery making in any shape or form should always
be enjoyable. I hope that *you* find making all of the
projects fun and that your appetite is wetted to
explore this fascinating activity further. It has
besotted me for the past twenty years and thankfully
shows no sign of letting up.

Happy potting!

The Principles
of Throwing

Creating beautiful thrown pottery at the wheel with
the confidence of a professional potter should be
within the reach of most pottery enthusiasts.
Throwing relies not only on skill and experience, but
on a thorough understanding of the different clays,
wheel types, tools and techniques. Truly expert
throwing can only be achieved once the essential
factors that have shaped the technique are
understood. I have always considered throwing to be
the most exciting of all pottery techniques, largely by
virtue of the demands it places on the potter and the
sense of personal achievement that comes
with success.

Clay manufacture and preparation

Although it is impossible to pinpoint the exact time at which the potter's wheel came into use, or indeed name its inventor, it is nevertheless generally accepted that by 2000 BC the wheel was being used widely and that it originated in Egypt. Prior to its introduction, functional pottery vessels were made using hand forming techniques, coiling being one of the most popular. It is easy to imagine how a potter creating a coil pot might have placed his clay on a surface which could be rotated to facilitate building the walls of the form. This could well have instigated the use of the wheel for throwing.

The invention of the wheel as a means of producing pottery enabled potters to increase their output dramatically. Throwing also promoted a fresh look at the possibilities of pottery design and a new subtlety of form emerged. Decorative devices based on drawing horizontal lines on to the revolving form became a recognizable feature of wheelthrown pottery and marked a move away from the more utilitarian ware of the past.

Refinements in the actual technique of throwing and improvements in wheel technology have advanced considerably over the years, but basic throwing techniques and the essential principle of the wheel have altered relatively little. In some countries today, primitive wheels are in everyday use and although they often comprise of little more than a heavy disc mounted on a fulcrum, rotated by hand or by foot, the craftsmanship of the vessels produced is quite remarkable. Although nowadays industrial manufacturing processes rely on jiggers and jolleys, casting and extrusion for their mass production, the wheel still seems to be as popular as ever. It enables the potter to make a wide variety of different forms relatively quickly compared to other hand forming pottery processes, and it never compromises individual creativity.

Throwing

Throwing is the process by which a wheelhead with variable rotational speeds is used to assist the hand forming of a homogeneous mass of soft plastic clay. Successful throwing is well within the reach of most people, but in common with all pottery techniques, success is not merely dependent on expertise. A good technique alone will not necessarily succeed if it is not put to use in conjunction with the correct type of clay. Throwing demands more from clay than any other pottery technique, because the clay must be suited to quick forming on the wheel; it must be sensitive enough to permit easy shaping; and at the same time it has to be rigid enough to ensure that the thrown form retains its shape while it is still wet.

Suitable throwing clays

Naturally occurring clays are numerous and vary enormously in appearance, chemical composition and in their behaviour during forming and firing. Nevertheless, all natural clays are classified into two categories: Primary and Secondary clays. This classification is based on whether the clay has been dug at its site of origin, when it is termed Primary, or whether it has since been transported to some other site by weathering elements and is therefore termed Secondary.

The purest clays are the primary clays, sometimes known as "residual". Not only does the action of the elements on the parent granite rock over the centuries serve to decompose the rock into clay, but also to transport the clay to other sites, often hundreds of miles away. China clay, or Kaolin, is the commonest form of primary clay. Deposits are found in and around granite outcrops.

Secondary clays are the most common of naturally occurring clays. Although these clays, like primary clays, originate from feldspathic rock, the transportation of the clay by rivers or glaciers and the effects of weathering alter the two most important characteristics of the clay. The particle size of secondary clay, which determines the "plasticity", or the suitability of a clay for use in pottery work, differentiates it from primary clay, as does the "contamination" by the variety of impurities it collects during its transportation.

Secondary differences

The size of the particles in secondary clay are smaller than those in primary clay, with the result that secondary clays are far more plastic. As the clay is transported from its site of origin, the particles are ground down. Running water is largely responsible for this grinding process, and it also sorts the particles into grades of fineness in a process known as "levigation". When particles of different sizes are carried along in flowing water, the larger, heavier particles settle first, leaving the finer grains suspended. It is usual, therefore, to find clays with a large particle formation on mature river beds, while those with fine particle formation are found some distance away, often deposited in lagoons or lakes. These clays are often referred to as being "sedimentary".

The impurities most commonly found in secondary clays are carbon material and iron oxide. Although carbon material within a clay may well affect its natural colour and assist plasticity, it burns away during the first firing. In some cases, a dark coloured clay will fire to a white or off-white colour. Iron oxide unless removed by special magnetic processes, remains in the clay throughout and affects the clay in terms of both its final fired colour, (clays with considerable iron content fire from a light tan to dark brown), and the maximum temperature it can withstand when fired. Iron oxide acts as a powerful flux in clays and as a result, many locally found clays with a high iron content cannot be fired to temperatures in excess of 1000 degrees. If they are, they begin to fuse and actually melt in a process called "vitrification" and the clay turns into a glass-like substance.

Preparation of secondary clays

The most common examples of secondary clay are ball clays, fireclays, and "brick clays" or marls. Naturally occurring clay is rarely in the right condition for throwing without further additions or blending. Most potters add to or alter secondary clay until they develop a clay that they can guarantee will behave in particular ways. Once a clay is treated to alter its natural characteristics, it is known as a "body". Although many experienced potters will prefer to develop specific clays themselves, specifically suited to their own needs, there is nothing to prevent potters with limited time or experience purchasing a manufactured ready-prepared body. I have used Potterycrafts "Throwers' Stoneware" clay for the projects in this book.

Apart from the mixing and blending of particular clays to obtain a body for successful throwing, fine sands and a material called "grog" are also added to improve the body's handling and firing characteristics. Grog is in fact clay that has been biscuit fired and then ground down to a particular grade of coarseness. The addition of sand or grog is usually undertaken to compensate for too much plasticity in a clay. Such clays are referred to as "fat" clays. If the clay is not plastic enough, it is termed "lean" or "short", and ball clay, which is highly plastic, is often added to remedy this deficiency.

The addition of sands and grog improves the working quality of over-plastic clay, increases its strength and gives it an open texture. This open texture allows the clay to dry more evenly, thus reducing the risk of warping or cracking. This process is known as giving the clay "bite" or "tooth". Because it has already been fired, the presence of grog within a clay also helps to minimize the shrinkage that occurs during firing when the water content of the clay is lost. The addition of grog also enables a clay to withstand highet temperatures. If a clay is not plastic enough, ball clay, which is highly plastic, can be added.

The clay manufacturing process

A raw clay is dug or mined and then crushed before being reduced to a liquid state called a "slip". A "blunger" is used to make slip. This machine works like a domestic food mixer, with a rotating blade in a tank breaking down the clay and mixing it with water until it becomes liquid. Blunged slip is then passed through special sieving screens which trap any unwanted materials such as grit and coarse sands. When a white body is required, slip can be passed across electro magnets which eliminate the iron content that would otherwise colour the clay.

The slip is then fed into a machine comprising of a series of large cloth bags. This is called a filter press. The water is squeezed out of the clay in this machine as the full bags of slip are mechanically pressed. The resulting cakes or slabs of clay are either allowed to dry, to be crushed at a later date and packaged as powdered clay or used as an additive in other clays, or they are kept in their plastic state and passed through a "pugmill". A pugmill is a long metal tube comprising a feed section, or "hopper", at one end, a middle section containing a powerful mixing blade, and a tapered end section that forces the clay to be compressed as it is extruded. The compression of the clay forces much of the air trapped within the clay to be expelled, but there are industrial pugmills available, called "de-airing" pugmills, which ensure that any air is completely removed.

Powdered or plastic clay?

Experienced studio potters usually develop their own personal body mixture so that they can guarantee that the clay they throw will behave in specific ways. It is obviously desirable to experiment with small amounts of raw materials when developing a new body and it is quite possible to mix powdered clays into a plastic consistency in much the same way as you would mix cement — on a clean floor using a shovel to turn the mixture and adding water to it gradually. Although time-consuming, mixing bodies from powder allows you to produce accurate clay combinations. It is also far more economical to buy clays in powder form.

The disadvantages of purchasing clays in powdered form are self-evident. For the beginner, or even the experienced potter who prefers the making process to preparation, being able to buy a plastic clay that needs relatively little further preparation prior to use can be cost effective. Consequently, most potters buy prepared clay in a plastic "ready-to-use" state, packed in 25kg (55lbs) blocks. Sand, grog, and other types of plastic clay can all be mixed into the clay, as described on p11.

Which clay to purchase

Although this book is concerned with throwing, it is important to consider various other important aspects of pottery before you choose your clay. Arguably, the most important of these is deciding to which temperature your work will need to be fired. Although a clay classified as stoneware (which can be fired to 1250–1300°C) can usually be fired at the lower temperature (900–1200°C) suited to earthenware, the reverse is not true. Some clays, particularly "red" clays cannot normally be fired at temperatures in excess of 1150°C without the risk of considerable warpage, bloating, or even melting.

Your choice of clay should also be determined by the final colour and texture you require. Your personal taste will obviously affect the type of pottery you want to produce, but factors such as the type of firing the clay is to receive should also be kept in mind when you choose your basic materials. The texture and colour of a piece of pottery will depend on whether it receives reduction or oxidised firing, and not just on the combination of clays in the body.

It is crucial to bear these considerations in mind when you are trying to choose the best clay for the type of work you plan to undertake. It is advisable to opt for a good general purpose throwing clay, at least to begin with. Look in manufacturers' catalogues for a clay suited to your needs – you may need one that is suited to throwing *and* hand forming for example. If you have attended pottery classes, find out from your tutor which clay you have been using and use this information as a guide when you come to buy your own. Most manufacturers sell their clays in small quantities as well as in bulk and, although expensive, small samples are ideal for experimenting with to discover which is the right clay body for your needs.

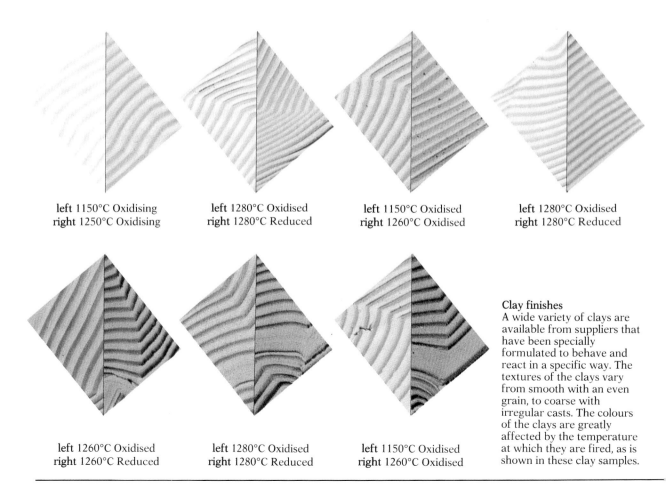

left 1150°C Oxidising
right 1250°C Oxidising

left 1280°C Oxidised
right 1280°C Reduced

left 1150°C Oxidised
right 1260°C Oxidised

left 1280°C Oxidised
right 1280°C Reduced

left 1260°C Oxidised
right 1260°C Reduced

left 1280°C Oxidised
right 1280°C Reduced

left 1150°C Oxidised
right 1260°C Oxidised

Clay finishes

A wide variety of clays are available from suppliers that have been specially formulated to behave and react in a specific way. The textures of the clays vary from smooth with an even grain, to coarse with irregular casts. The colours of the clays are greatly affected by the temperature at which they are fired, as is shown in these clay samples.

Clay preparation

Good throwing requires more than merely finding a good throwing clay and developing a successful throwing technique. The clay has to be in good working condition, or "well-prepared", before you can think about beginning to throw, since throwing demands a high quality clay.

A well-prepared clay should be of an even, soft consistency, have an evenly distributed water content and be free of any air pockets. Although bought plastic clay is described by its manufacturers as being ready to use, it will undoubtedly need further preparation – at the very least it should be passed through a pugmill. If you do not have access to a pugmill, you will need to imitate its effects by "wedging" and "kneading" the clay. Some potters only feel happy with their clay when they have continued to wedge and knead it even after it has been pugged.

Wedging

Wedging ensures that the clay is well mixed and also helps to expel any pockets of air which may be present. Small amounts of clay can be "hand-wedged", which simply entails breaking the clay into two, holding the pieces of clay in each hand and smacking them together smartly with force.

This kind of hand-wedging is obviously not practical when you are dealing with large pieces of clay. Wedging large weights of clay involves slamming the whole piece down with considerable, but controlled, force from head height on to a concrete slab positioned at waist height. Once it has been slammed down, the lump of clay should be turned longways and cut in half. One half of the clay is then slammed down from a height on to the other half; this new lump is in turn dissected and one half is slammed down on to the other. This halving and rejoining is repeated until the clay is well mixed and cutting the block in half does not reveal air pockets.

Clay should be wedged until it is quite soft but not sticky. Although you cannot over-wedge clay, wedging does tend to dry clay out and stiffen it. For this reason, bear in mind that the clay you are preparing may need redamping before successful throwing is possible.

1 Hold a piece of clay in both hands at head height and then slam it down with some force on to the concrete slab. Lift the clay and having turned it through 90°, slam it down again. Repeat this process once more.

2 Turn the block of clay lengthways on the slab and slice across it with a cutting wire. Lift one half of this block and slam it down on top of the other. Dissect the clay and re-wedge it.

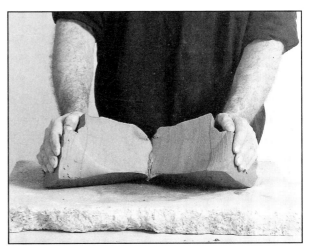

3 Repeat this slicing in half and rejoining until the clay is thoroughly mixed. If you see any air pockets in the cut surface of the clay, wedge the block again and continue to do so until all the air is expelled.

Kneading

Kneading should take place while the clay is still soft. The two basic methods of kneading take their names from the shape of the clay they create: the "ram" or "bullshead" method and the "spiral kneading" method. Spiral kneading is the best technique to use when preparing large amounts of clay. Downward, forward pressure is exerted on the mass with your strongest hand while you hold, lift and pivot the clay mass on the spot with the other. This serves to offer the next part of the clay to your compressing hand. The action develops a spiral shape in the clay being worked. ▽

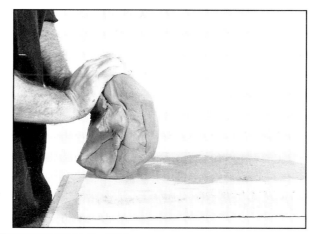

1 The "oxhead" method is probably the easier to grasp, because it imitates the action we associate with kneading dough, although conversely the intention is to expel air. Place your hands close together on the lump of clay and push down and away from your body using the palms of your hands.

2 As the clay spreads away from you, pull the far edge back to the centre in a rhythmic rocking motion. Press down again on the clay that has been pulled back on itself and repeat the process. Spreading the clay over the working surface mixes it and the downward pressure expels any trapped air.

3 The kneaded clay will ultimately look like the head of a bull as a result of this rolling action. Kneading, like wedging, mixes the clay and ensures that it has no air pockets by virtue of the continuous compressing action it involves. ▷

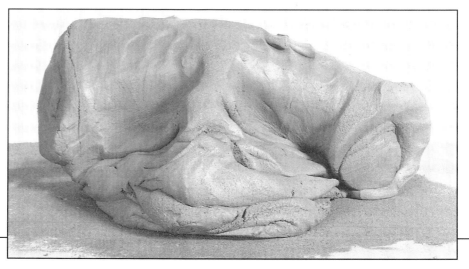

Reclaiming clay

The clay you have to work with may not be in the best condition for throwing. Clay that has dried out too much to use, unfired scraps of clay, and unprocessed clay, can all be reclaimed to use for throwing. Place the clay in a watertight container and pour enough water into it to cover the clay. Leave the clay until it breaks down into a slurry, or has "slaked down". The clay will settle to the bottom of the container. Drain the excess water away. If you are preparing locally dug clay that may have impurities in it, you should pass the slurry through a coarse sieve to remove these foreign bodies.

Remove the slurry from the container and spread it out on a plaster slab or wooden boards so it can begin to dry out. Once the clay has dried sufficiently to be handled without too much of it sticking to your hands, it can be kneaded and wedged ready for use.

Adding other materials to clay

It is often desirable, and in some instances advisable, to add other ingredients or dry materials to plastic clay. Sand or grog are quite common additives which alter the clay's texture as well as its handling characteristics and its final temperature tolerance. In order to mix these into the clay thoroughly while the clay is in its plastic state, the clay mass should be cut into slices, the sand or grog sprinkled between the layers, and then the clay should be kneaded and wedged. Adding dry material to clay dries it out, so additions should be made preferably when the clay is still quite soft.

If colours, in the form of oxide powders or body stains, are to be added to a clay, it is best to mix them with a little water to form a paste. This paste is spread over the slices of clay prior to kneading and wedging. This ensures that the colour is distributed evenly through the clay.

Clay storage

Once clay has been prepared, some form of storage is required that will keep it in prime working condition. Many potters prefer to leave their clay to "age" or "sour" once it has been prepared in order for it to be in peak condition when they come to work with it. Ageing clay simply means that clay in its plastic state is left for a period of time to settle, while souring involves the organic activity of injected bacteria on the clay substance. Although the purist might well insist that clay should be left to age or sour before it is ready to use, very few aspiring potters have the facilities to store large amounts of clay in order to undertake the processes properly. Luckily, bought plastic clays can be used successfully with the minimum of preparation. In any event, putting clay through a pugmill is considered an effective way to prepare it to the same degree as one month's ageing.

It is the moisture content of a clay that determines its working plasticity so it is very important to prevent water evaporation during storage. Clay manufacturers sell plastic clay in tough polythene sacks and as long as these sacks are not torn, the clay can be kept indefinitely if the sacks are stored in a cool damp environment. Although the effect of frost eventually increases the plasticity of clay, it is a great enemy to any potter trying to store these plastic sacks of clay. Frost tears the polythene sacks causing the clay to spill out, and its initial effect on the clay means that it will need considerable kneading and wedging if it is to be used successfully.

It is always advisable to ensure that sufficient clay is prepared in advance of a throwing session so that your throwing is not interrupted. Smaller quantities of prepared clay are more practical for day-to-day use, and are best stored in plastic bins, with airtight lids. Clay dries out quickly in the warm environment of a studio, so it is advisable not to leave your clay supply exposed during a throwing session.

Having to stop in mid-flow is counterproductive, and if a pugmill is not available, preparing large quantities of clay is both time and energy consuming.

The wheel and the thrower's tools

The most basic potter's wheel is simply a flat turntable fixed to a vertical shaft. The ways in which the shaft causes the turntable, or wheelhead, to rotate and the methods used to power the mechanism have developed over the years to produce a wide range of wheel types. Nevertheless, these wheel types can be roughly categorized into three groups: the "direct kick" wheels; the "treadle kick" wheels; and the electric wheels.

The direct kick wheel consists of a large fly wheel that is rotated by hand or foot. The wheel relies on the weight of the fly wheel to provide a period of continuous rotational momentum during which throwing can take place. The disadvantage of this type of wheel is that it is difficult to control or greatly vary the speed at which it rotates. The treadle kick wheel can be seen as the logical development from the direct kick wheel. The main difference between the two is that instead of kicking the flywheel directly, the potter uses a foot-operated treadle to control its momentum. Wheels of this type are available with either front or side treadles. The front treadle style is operated in a standing position and has a very lightweight flywheel, making it tiring to try and maintain a constant speed for any length of time. This type of wheel is often the cheapest, but its use is limited; beginners especially will find it very frustrating trying to balance on one foot, treadle steadily with the other *and* think carefully about their throwing technique. The best style of treadle wheel is one with the treadle step at the side, such as the David Leach kick wheel. These wheels usually have a flywheel that is sufficiently heavy to maintain a good rotational momentum without excessive effort. They are also operated from a seated position, which eliminates the problems of stance and stability.

Personal preference coupled with many years of teaching has led me to believe that the electric wheel is by far the best option. Although they are more expensive than kick wheels, electric wheels are easy to use and demand the minimum of physical effort. The purist might argue that the electric wheel does not allow for the same sensitivity of control that the kick wheel provides, but this minor drawback is compensated for by the ease with which the electric wheel can reach a range of speeds and maintain them indefinitely. Once you have bought your wheel, it will require very little maintenance to keep it in good working order.

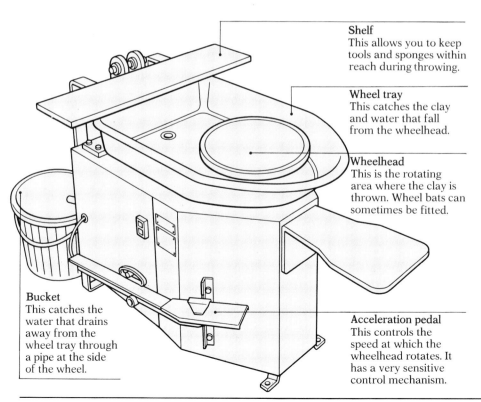

Shelf
This allows you to keep tools and sponges within reach during throwing.

Wheel tray
This catches the clay and water that fall from the wheelhead.

Wheelhead
This is the rotating area where the clay is thrown. Wheel bats can sometimes be fitted.

Bucket
This catches the water that drains away from the wheel tray through a pipe at the side of the wheel.

Acceleration pedal
This controls the speed at which the wheelhead rotates. It has a very sensitive control mechanism.

The electric wheel
There are many different types of electric wheel on the market. It can often be more practical to opt for a cheaper model, so that you can buy all the equipment you need, rather than choose the most expensive. A variety of different systems are used to transfer the motored rotation to the wheelhead — cone systems, variable pulleys, friction wheels and variable transformers to name but a few. The crucial thing to bear in mind when choosing a wheel is that it should have a good range of speeds, and will slow down whatever the speed setting or size of clay being thrown. A mistake often made by new potters is to buy a wheel that suits their initial capabilities, and then discover that this wheel does not function efficiently when their range increases.

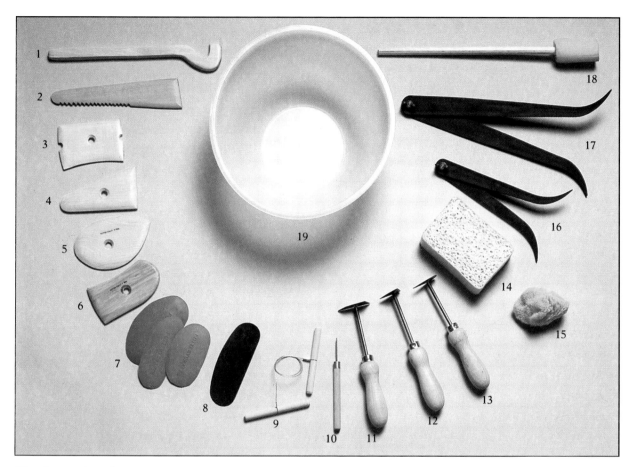

The thrower's tools

The only absolutely essential items needed by a potter are a wheel, clay, water and his hands. There are, however, several tools which assist the throwing process considerably and every potter quickly accumulates a range of items that become personal essentials.

I feel that the most important aid to successful throwing is the removable wheel bat. Although wheel bats may technically constitute equipment rather than tools, I have included them in my discussion of the tools because I see them as an invaluable help when removing large or delicate pieces of work from the wheelhead. If you cannot afford a special system as such, you can make your own by setting two studs into the wheelhead and boring two locating holes through several wooden wheel bats that correspond to the position of these studs. It is essential to ensure that the studs do not protrude above the level of the wood. It is very simple to increase a wheel bat's use further by drawing on several concentric rings: these make invaluable guidelines during turning when accurate re-centring is essential, *(see p26)*.

1-8: Throwing ribs are useful for shaping, smoothing and steadying thrown shapes. A variety of shapes are available in wood, but rubber and metal kidneys can be used for the same purpose.

9: Cutting wire to cut pots from the wheelhead. Twisted wires produce a pleasing shell pattern on the pot base.

10: Needles, preferably set into handles, for trimming off any unevenness from rims.

11: Turning tools are used for paring away unwanted clay from the base of thrown forms, both directly after throwing is completed and at the leather hard stage when the pot is inverted on the wheelhead for turning to take place. These tools are available with a variety of differently shaped working edges. The most commonly used are rectangular, triangular and pear-shaped, but it is always useful to build up a range of shapes.

14,15: Large synthetic sponges for mopping out the wheel tray and general cleaning and small natural sponges for smoothing off finished thrown forms.

16,17: Calipers for recording measurements of rim diameters for lid fittings and other necessary dimensions.

18: Sponge stick for mopping out water from the inside base of tall or narrow-necked forms.

19: Bowls are required to hold the water necessary to lubricate the clay.

Centring

Centring is the process which ensures that the clay is revolving in the centre of the wheelhead. It is the key to successful throwing. All potters eventually develop their own pet throwing techniques to achieve specific results, and by the same token centring is undertaken by different potters in very different ways. Nevertheless, although techniques may differ, the principle remains the same — to align a piece of clay in the exact centre of the wheelhead before throwing begins. I have described several different hand positions for the final stage of centring, which can be adapted until you find the centring position that is most comfortable and successful for you.

Centring is arguably the most important aspect of throwing, because until you have mastered the technique it is unlikely that you will be able to throw effectively. The results of throwing from an uncentred block of clay include walls of uneven thickness, weak spots, and poor and unstable shapes.

1 It is always best to use soft well-prepared clay to practise centring. Block the clay into a ball and slam it down on to the wheelhead, placing it as centrally as possible. Pat the block into a round domed shape. Make sure you are comfortably seated.

2 Use the edge of the wheel tray to steady your arms as you lean over the wheelhead. Lubricate your hands and the clay with plenty of water. During centring, try to ensure that your hands are linked together for steadiness.

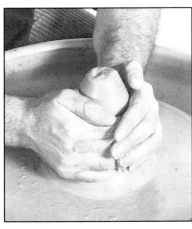

3 Imagine that the circle of the wheelhead is a clock face and place your arms at about twenty past seven. Use pressure from the outer edge of the palms of both hands to force the clay up into a cone.

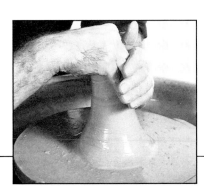

4 Bring the cone down again by cupping its apex with your right hand, supporting the sides of the form and this hand with your left hand. Repeat the process several times. Coning helps to move the clay into the centre of the wheelhead; it distributes moisture evenly through the clay; and it disperses any air pockets.

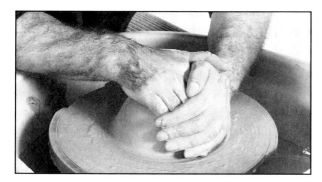

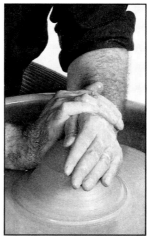

5 │ The clay should now be nearly centred. There are several final centring positions. Place your arms at half past eight on the wheelhead and cup the clay with both hands. The fingertips of your right hand should touch the surface of the wheel, while your left hand acts as a support. Press down on the clay with your right hand, while pulling towards you simultaneously with your left.

6 │ With your arms in the same position, apply pressure with your left hand while pushing away from you with your right. Grip your left wrist with your right hand for support.

7 │ Again, with your arms in the same position, press down on to the clay with the outer edge of your right hand while pushing away with your left.

8 │ Always leave the surface of the clay very gradually — sudden movements may throw the clay off centre. Check that the clay is accurately centred by touching the side of the dome lightly with the point of a tool. If the clay is centred, the circumference line will appear without a break or any unevenness. As your experience increases, you will know instinctively when the clay is correctly centred.

A Cylinder

The two most important basic throwing techniques are employed when making the cylinder and the shallow open form. For a cylinder, begin by practising with small pieces of clay; as your expertise increases, use larger amounts. This step-by-step outline is based on throwing 3.5kg (7lbs) of clay, but 1kg (2lbs) is a good weight with which to practise.

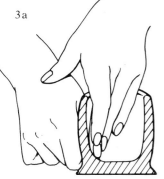

1 Press your thumb into the centred clay to a level about 2 cm (³/₄in) above the wheelhead. Support the outer surface of the clay with your left hand and brace your arms against the wheel tray for steadiness. Form the inner base by pushing your thumb out towards the fingers of your right hand. Use your left hand to support the outer wall. △

2 With the clay gripped between your thumb and first finger, keep a constant but gentle pressure and steadily raise the wall to increase the height of the cylinder. ◁

3a

3 During subsequent lifts of the wall, you will find it necessary to substitute the initial lifting grip of thumb and first finger with one that involves both hands. This change becomes necessary when you can no longer reach the surface of the inner base with your thumb. Lift the outer wall with the inner side of your right hand, holding it clenched slightly to form a fist. Support the inner wall with your left hand, pressing with your middle finger against the lifting action of your right.

4 It is important that the lift is a directly vertical one or the shape will flare outwards. You may find it easier to stand leaning over the wheelhead and guide the clay up from that perspective. It is also very important to keep the pressure between your hands constant. If it alters, the form may develop a twist or tilt off balance and the wall may even tear. △

5 Reduce the speed of the wheel and collar the cylinder with steady pressure from both hands. This will steady the clay in readiness for further lifts. To ensure steadiness throughout the throwing process, either rest your forearms on the wheel tray or tuck your elbows into your sides. Movement is minimalised because it derives purely from your linked hands.

6 Trim the edge of the rim with a needle. Hold the needle in your right hand and steady the inside of the form with your left, at the point where the clay will be cut. Push the needle into the clay and rotate the wheel slowly. When the needle meets your finger on the inside of the cylinder, lift off the loop of clay. ▷

7 Gently compress the rim to both flatten and thicken it. Use a throwing rib or a suitable turning tool to gently compress the wall of the cylinder for greater stability. Support the inner wall with your left hand as you do so. △

8 Mop out any water remaining inside the cylinder with a sponge attached to a stick. Trim away any excess clay from around the base.▽

How to identify faults

The most common cause of problems when throwing a cylinder is initial inaccuracy in the centring of the clay. If, however, a cylinder develops a swelling midway up its side or in its upper section, the chances are that you are not lifting it vertically and are therefore allowing the walls to flare out, or that your fingers are incorrectly positioned during the lift. If you are exerting pressure with the fingers of your left hand at a point either above or below the corresponding pressure exerted by your right hand, the shape will flare at that point, (see Swelling p23).

If the clay wall tears during a lift, it is usually a result of trying to lift too much in one go and applying too much pressure. Alternatively it could be because you have suddenly increased the pressure at one point. Tearing can also result from lack of lubrication – your hands will stick to the clay if it is too dry and distort or tear it.

A shallow open form

The open form is probably the easiest shape to begin throwing, because the centrifugal force of the rotating wheel almost wills the clay to open out once you start the process. Throwing the cylinder, on the other hand, demands that this tendency to open out be contained and redirected in a vertical direction to give the form height.

1 | Centre the clay and spread it out on the wheelhead to form a flattened shape, using the palm of your right hand to press the clay down. Support the widening rim of the clay with your left hand. The area of the wheelhead that the clay covers will determine the width of the base. The maximum diameter of the form can only be a little more than this if the wall is to remain stable. ◁

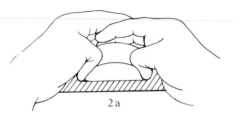

2 a

2 | Form a small well in the centre of the clay with the tip of your right thumb to a level about 2cm (³⁄₄in) above the wheelhead. Add a little water to the well and place both thumbs inside it. Push both thumbs outwards in opposite directions, supporting the clay with your palms. As the form opens out, maintain a steady pressure on the rim with the inside edge of your thumb to prevent it from splitting. ▷

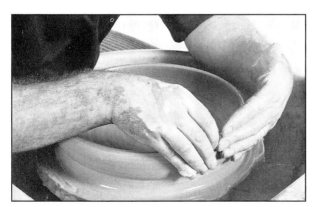

3 | Once the diameter of the wall extends the base by about 3cm (1¹⁄₅in), remove any water from the inside of the form with a sponge while it is still rotating. If the wall is thick enough, raise it slightly using your thumb and middle finger. The rim can be compressed to flatten it and if you wish you can also indent it to make it a decorative feature. △

4 | Remove some of the excess clay from around the base with a turning tool, ensuring that enough clay is left to maintain the stability of the shape. Cut the shape from the wheelhead with a cutting wire and remove it when it has stiffened, (*see "Removing work from the wheel", p32*).

Swelling

The centrifugal force of the rotating wheelhead encourages thrown forms to open or swell with the minimum of assistance. Consequently the potter is actively engaged in preventing this from happening rather than encouraging it.

When the swelling of a form is required in a controlled manner, however, it is undertaken either as a part of the lifting or raising process, or once any lifting has been completed. Ideally it should begin from the very first lift – the final swell being determined by the tendency of the emerging wall. The final shape only then needs slight modification or refinement towards the end of the throwing process.

1 The forming of a bowl shape shows the swelling technique most clearly since both lifting and swelling occur simultaneously. Begin to develop a gradual swell with your first lift. This is especially important when you are throwing large forms whose stability relies on very gradual and careful swelling. ▷

2 During swelling, pressure should be exerted from within the form with the fingers of your left hand, with your right hand providing support as well as lifting. Further lifting and swelling requires the same hand action. The thickness of clay is now used to swell the shape rather than extend the height of the wall. ▷

3 Modifications in shape can be made using the fingertips of both hands. Any further shaping can take place from within the form. Many potters prefer to use a sponge or a rubber kidney or a rib rather than their fingers. Whenever you are throwing, establish a comfortable, steady position to work from. ◁

4 When you work with small shapes, pressure is still exerted from within, but you may only need the thumb and middle fingers of your right hand to swell the clay. Your left hand acts as a support. △

5 When a shallow swelled form is required, such as in the making of a domed lid, both hands work to produce a lifting and swelling action. Here once again the pressure is exerted from inside the form with the fingers of your right hand steadying and assisting the lifting action.

Collaring

1 Collaring produces a compression of the clay that both thickens and steadies the wall. Consequently, even when you are throwing a straightish cylinder, a very gentle collaring action may be advisable as you raise the shape to stabilize and compress the walls. △

Collaring, or throttling as it is sometimes known, is the term applied to the technique used to restrict or narrow the shape of a form. The action employed in this technique involves gripping the clay with your hands as if you were strangling it. Pressure is applied inwards through both hands as they collar over the specific area to be narrowed. Collaring demands far more from the potter and the clay than does swelling, for instance, because trying to restrict or narrow the shape works against the tendency of the clay to open out as the wheel rotates. It should be carried out in gradual stages with the shape being coaxed rather than forced inwards. The wheel should be rotating at a medium speed and pressure should be exerted in a gentle, determined fashion. During throwing, the ultimate form of any shape should be kept in mind from the start. If a form needs to be tapered or narrow at a particular point, this shaping should occur gradually. Only last minute refinements should be necessary when lifting is completed.

2 When a rounded or completely enclosed shape is being made, we can see quite clearly how pressure from within swells the wall and how pressure from without closes it over. The passive hand is used as a means of steadying the wall as it is manipulated to the desired shape. △

3 Narrowing a shape produces a compressed, thickened section in the clay. This thickening can be used to produce shapes which might otherwise have proved difficult to throw — a round-bellied form with a long narrow neck for example. The neck area is defined by collaring after an initial lift, leaving the neck section thick so that further lifting can take place without altering the shape of the lower section. Repeated collaring allows for more shaping. △

4 Collaring can also be used to produce interesting design effects during throwing. Collaring at intervals up the wall of any shape will alter its silhouette in an unusual way. The extra thickness around the rim area of thrown forms in which collaring results is put to good use when making forms, such as teapots, that require an internal gallery. These galleries can be created easily from the extra thickness of clay. ◁

Rims

The rim of a form, like any other part of it, plays an important part in determining the quality of its final appearance. The most essential requirement of any rim, regardless of its style, is that it should appear to be an integral part of the potter's overall design. Very often, beginners fail to work on the rims of pots they throw with as much energy as the rest of the form, with the result that their rims detract from the overall look of their work. The final shaping of the rim may well be determined to a large extent by the function the form is designed to fulfill, but in any event the design of a form should live in harmony with and enhance its function. All the forces exerted in the lifting of walls during throwing flow upwards, so any unevenness or movement off-centre will manifest themselves mainly at the rim. Trimming off any unevenness with a needle allows for the final shaping of the rim to take place with a clean, even result. Rims can be thick or thin, simple or complex in shape, and it is quite possible to alter the nature of a rim completely to suit a particular requirement, as long as the walls of the form are not too thin. Ideally you should plan the rim as an integral part of the whole shape before you begin to throw, so that it emerges as a natural progression of the form. A simple but useful exercise to undertake is to throw a number of similar cylinders with different rims and see how a different rim affects the look of a pot.

1 To make a thickened, slightly sloping rim, first trim off any uneveness and then, supporting the inside and outside of the shape apply pressure to the rim. This compression can be continued for as long as is necessary to produce a slanted surface to the rim.

2 A compressed rim can be split quite simply using your thumb nail to add interest and texture to a piece of pottery.

3 Applying pressure downwards on the inside of a rim, forcing the clay to slope down and inwards produces a very clean outer edge and gives the pot a modern feel.

4 To produce a flared rim, gently bend the edge of the rim outwards. The edge can be left quite angular on a large flared rim, or extended to be really fine and simple.

5 A tapered rim can be produced by collaring and shaping the sloped surface. Continued shaping can produce unusual rims, with flat inner edges or softened edges.

6 The shape of the rim can be altered by manipulating its edge as if a series of spouts were to be made. This gives the pot a crinkled, and highly textured edge.

Turning

Turning, or trimming, is the process by which excess or unwanted clay is removed from the outer base edge and the underside of a thrown form when it has dried to leather hard. It should not be necessary for turning to be performed on the inside or the rim of a form because these areas should be finished during the actual throwing process. The most important reason for turning is an aesthetic one. Apart from altering the ultimate profile of a shape, turning also allows excess weight to be removed, giving a form the right "feel" in relation to its size.

It is always desirable, however, to keep turning to the minimum. It should be looked upon as a means of adding a final correction to a form, rather than as a means of radically altering its shape. When it is leather hard, clay loses the ability it had during throwing to respond to pressure in a fluid way. Many potters argue that, with the exception of spherical shapes, flat dishes and bowls, which are virtually impossible to throw without leaving a ridge of surplus clay around their base, very little if any turning should be required if a shape has been well thrown.

Turning should only affect the base section of a thrown form. Because the thickness of clay at the base of any form is relatively great, the base area always takes longer to dry than the rest of the form. For this reason, once a piece of work is dry enough to handle without fear of deforming its shape, it should be turned upside down to ensure that the piece dries evenly. Removing thrown pieces from the wheelhead and placing them on paper-covered boards to dry ensures that their bases are not distorted, because they are easily removed from the board without needing to be released with a wire; this clean base cut assists easy turning.

Another way to assist turning is to make a conscious effort to keep the thickness of the bases of the forms you throw constant. A thickness of about 2cm (³/₄in) is usually suitable for most items. If you are sure of the amount of clay on the base you have to work with, you will be able to gauge how deeply you can trim the base without the constant worry of breaking through the clay shell.

Pots should be trimmed when they are leather hard, because at that stage of drying, the clay can be pared off cleanly. If you trim a pot when it is too damp, the clay trimmings will stick to the sides of the form; if you leave a pot too long, turning will take much longer and the clay will come away as a crumbly powder.

Re-centring

Just as good throwing depends on the clay being centred accurately, successful turning depends on accurate re-centring. It is impossible to re-centre a pot that was thrown when wrongly centred, but you can turn an "off-centred" pot if you concentrate on re-centring its base rather than its rim. Metal wheelheads have concentric rings marked into their surface which can be used to help you re-centre your work. If you are using a wooden removable wheel bat, it is well worth drawing such a guide on to it with a pencil.

1 Simply rotate the wheel slowly and hold a pencil to it to mark out several concentric widths. A pot that was well-centred initially can be easily re-centred using the rings as a guide and will require only slight adjustments. Check that your work is centred accurately by holding a tool steadily against the surface of the form as it rotates. △

2 If the line produced on the form is uneven or broken, re-align your work away from the point where the tool has cut most deeply into the clay. If the line is constant and of an even depth, the pot is centred and you can secure it to the wheelhead. ▷

Turning priorities

A comfortable position at the wheel and body steadiness are as important during turning as during throwing. Whenever possible, rest your forearms on the wheeltray. Turning is best performed with your arms held at half past three on an imaginary clockface. Try to support your trimming hand with your left to provide maximum stability.

The footring is an important feature of any piece and should be considered in advance. The shape and size of a footring will depend on the type of form you throw, but it is always useful to form it so that you can grip it easily with one hand. You will then be able to dip the form in its glaze without losing your grip on its base. ▷

The most common problems to arise during turning are associated with the pot having been incorrectly centred, or with the clay being in the wrong condition to work with. "Chattering" may occur, when the surface of the clay develops ripples, either because the clay is too dry to turn, because you are holding the tool too loosely, or because the tool is not sharp enough. Pots thrown from clays with a heavy grog content will often develop horizontal scratches across their surface. These scratch lines can be eliminated by smoothing with a rubber kidney, a wooden tool or a throwing rib as the wheel rotates.

Not all thrown shapes are stable when inverted, however, and some require special supports during turning. Large bowls with diameters wider than that of the wheelhead, rounded pots with very small necks and pots with long narrow necks all need these supports, or "chucks" as they are known. A chuck can be made from thickly thrown collars of clay that have been left to dry to leather hard. Alternatively, there are many objects that can be used as chucks, such as plastic plant pots, plastic bowls or lengths of sturdy cardboard tubing. Such chucks benefit from the addition of a coil of soft clay around their rims, to cushion the inverted pots.

Turning long-stemmed forms

For a chuck, use a length of sturdy tubing cut so as to prevent any weight pressing on to the fragile lip of the carafe. Alternatively, you could throw a clay chuck. Centre the chuck and secure it to the wheelhead with small pieces of clay. To cushion the inverted carafe, smooth a thick coil of clay around the lip of the chuck and down over the sides. Trim the upper rim of the cushion level with a pin. Trim the base of the carafe and finish in the usual way.

1 Begin the turning process by levelling the base of the form. Brace your arms against your sides. Start at the centre and lightly pare off the clay in even whorls, moving your turning tool out towards the edge. This will remove any unevenness.

2 Trim away any ragged clay from the edge before you define the footring. Trim the outside of the pot to the required profile and define the area in which you want to form the footring. Work from the centre to the inner side of the footring area.

3 Work from the outer side of the footring down over the edge of the base. Pare away the clay gently, resisting the temptation to apply more pressure, which could cause the tool to become embedded in the clay, pushing the pot off-centre or dislodging it.

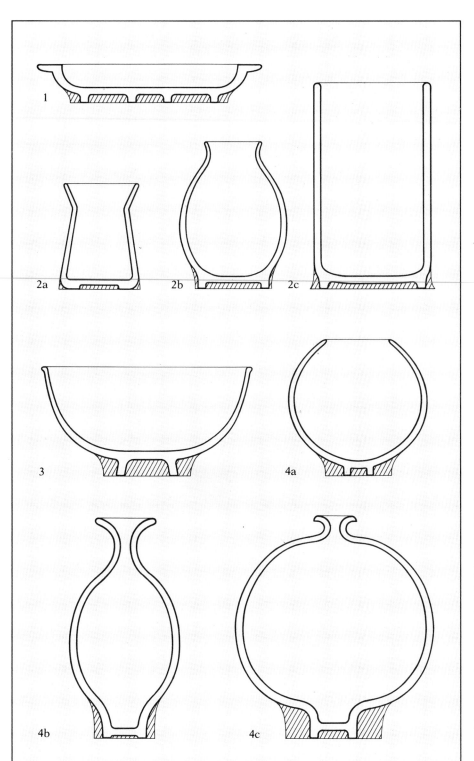

Footrings
These cross-sectional drawings show the shapes of various turned footrings, together with the quantity of clay that has to be trimmed away. Wide dishes require a double footring to prevent sagging *(1)*, while narrower cylindrical forms need only a small amount of trimming to be fully stable, *(2)*. Ideally, footrings should be made so that they are easy to grip when the form is inverted during glazing, *(3)*. Large shapes with swollen bellies should be thrown with relatively thick bases to be stable, and their footrings will therefore need to be trimmed quite substantially before they attain their intended shape, *(4)*.